FLING, SLING AND BATTER YOUR WAY TO VICTORY

to surrender. If refused, the attackers would try to starve the defenders into submission. If this didn't work, they would try to take the castle by force. Weapons they used to blast holes in the castle's defences included siege engines such as battering rams, trebuchets and catapults ...

Contents

Castle under siege

Imagine a medieval siege. Towering walls are battered by gigantic catapults. Deadly arrows fly through the air. The purpose? To capture an enemy castle by cutting off its supplies. Between the years 1000 and 1470, powerful kings, queens and nobles built big castles across Europe and the Middle East. They grew rich from taxes and trade. Whoever held the castle, controlled the land and the people.

The town gathers supplies

For days before the siege, rebel knights and soldiers would hurry into the castle. Defences would be mended, weapons prepared, and carts of grain taken from the surrounding villages. At the start of the siege, the attackers would set up camp, surrounding the castle with troops so that no one could get in or out.

Evolution of castles

Over the ages, castle builders updated designs to offer better protection from attack. Timber, which could be burnt down, was replaced by rings of thick stone walls. Square towers were replaced by round ones. Gatehouses were strengthened and fitted with traps and other cunning defences.

Advantages and disadvantages: →

The attackers arrive

Attackers could block the channel that carried fresh spring water into the castle and its town. If the defenders were lucky, there would be deep wells inside the castle walls, so their water supplies would not run out.

Spear

Pole axe

Moat

Drawbridge

Knights

Camp

Walls

Crossbowman

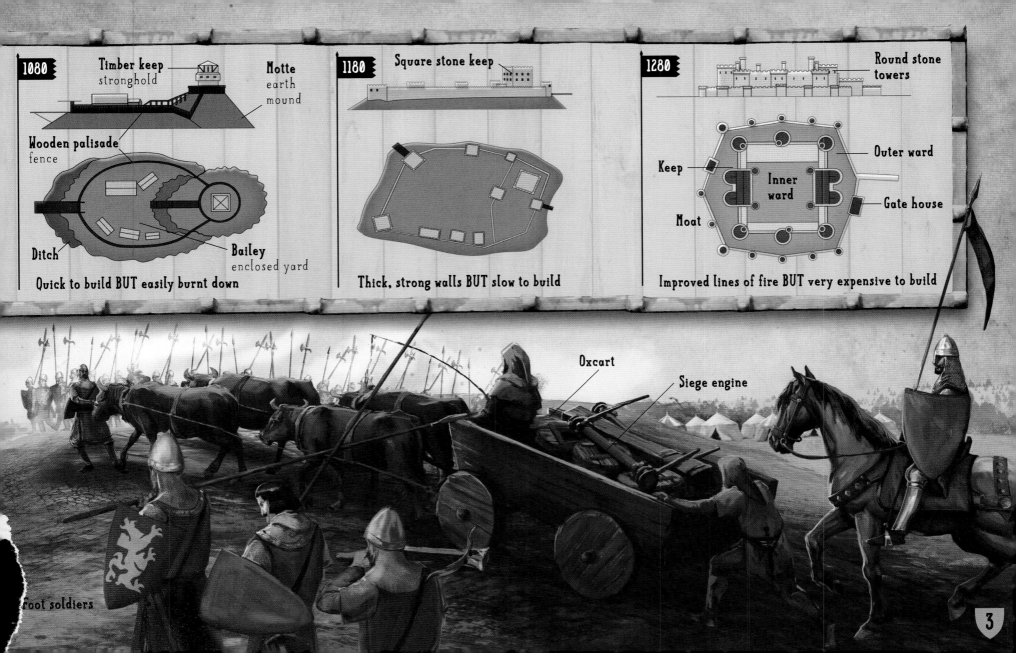

1080
Timber keep
stronghold

Motte
earth
mound

Wooden palisade
fence

Ditch

Bailey
enclosed yard

Quick to build BUT easily burnt down

1180
Square stone keep

Thick, strong walls BUT slow to build

1280
Round stone
towers

Keep

Inner
ward

Outer ward

Gate house

Moat

Improved lines of fire BUT very expensive to build

Oxcart

Siege engine

foot soldiers

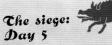
Mud, blood and stone

The walls around the town and the castle were joined. Soldiers patrolled the walkways. Within the castle was a central stronghold called the keep. Around it were courtyards, walls within walls, low towers and high towers. The appearance of the castle was meant to strike fear into any enemy!

Attacking foot soldiers

Most foot soldiers wore a padded or leather tunic. Some wore mail or pieces of plate armour, and often a metal helmet. Some carried a spear or a sword, or had a pole arm, such as a halberd or glaive. These were weapons with a blade fixed at the end of a long wooden shaft.

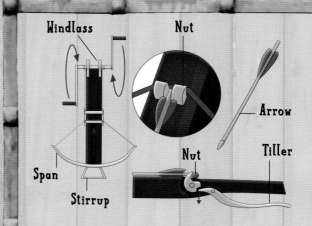

Crossbow

Crossbows or arbalests were in use from the 1060s to the 1500s. All sorts of mechanisms were invented to pull back the string to give maximum firepower.

Iron helmet

Quilted armour

Large shield

Longbow

Pole axe

Kettle helmet

4

Arrow storm

Huge numbers of arrows were made before a siege or a battle. Attacking archers took up positions behind large shelters called mantlets, or body-sized shields called pavises. They used longbows to target men on the castle walls, or shot blazing arrows at the wooden hoardings in the hope of starting a fire.

Hoarding

Pavise

Crossbow

The soldier behind the pavise is rewinding his crossbow. A powerful weapon, it fires a bolt that can punch its way through plate armour – but it is slower to re-load than a longbow.

Crossbow

Hoarding

The defenders built a wooden gallery along the tops of the walls and towers. It was called a hoarding, and it made it easier for defenders to shoot arrows at the enemy, or drop rocks on their heads.

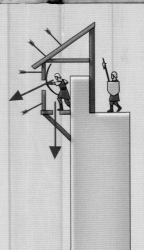

The Earl ordered us to prepare the siege engines for an assault, but at first light 13 rebel knights galloped out from the castle and attacked our camp. They slaughtered our guards and scattered the campfires, setting alight tents and the catapult timbers. We pulled three of the knights off their horses, but the others made it back into the castle under a hail of arrows.

Knights in armour

Knights were soldiers on horseback. During the Middle Ages they became elite troops with a high-ranking position in society. In an open battle the knights would lead a deadly charge, breaking up the enemy lines. During a siege, knights from the castle might launch a surprise attack on the enemy.

Surprise attack

Clattering hooves, armour and swords! Defending knights sometimes carried out a daring counter-attack called a sortie. They would leave the castle through a secret gate, called a sally-port or postern, and take the enemy camp by surprise.

Battle axe

Shoulder guards

Wooden shield

| Bend | Per pale indented | Barry | Paly |

Heraldry

During the fighting, a knight used his shield for defence or as a weapon. The pattern on the shield was a sort of family badge, which identified the owner. Use of these patterns and emblems, many of which had names, is called heraldry.

Mace

Broad sword

Stakes to
protect ground
army from
cavalry

Great helm

War horse

The knight's life often
depended on a good war
horse. Stirrups and a
raised saddle helped him
to stay on his horse when
he struck the enemy with
his lance, or slashed
with his sword.

1100 →   1280 →

1380 →   1450 →

Changing armour

In the 1100s, knights' armour was made of
mail. In the 1220s knights began to protect
their knees with plates of solid metal. By
the 1350s plate armour covered the legs,
arms and other parts of the body, too.
During the 1400s, metal armour covered a
knight's entire body.

The waiting game

The rules of war allowed the two sides in a battle or siege to stop fighting and have a discussion, or parley. The attackers generally preferred to capture a castle that was in good working order, rather than one they had just battered to bits. That was why they often agreed not to kill the defenders if they surrendered peacefully. A long siege could end in death and destruction.

Treachery

Attackers tried to find secret ways into the castle. They bribed local people for useful information about tunnels, shafts or hidden gates.

The 'sow'

Undermining a wall

Attackers often tried to undermine the castle. They dug a tunnel under the wall and used wooden props to hold up the tunnel roof. At the last minute, the miners set these wooden props on fire and made their escape. Their plan was that the props would burn through, the tunnel would collapse, and the wall above fall down.

Wooden supports set on fire

Tunnel

Filling the drained moat

Archers shot from the battlements. Here they are aiming at the attackers below, who are trying to drain part of the moat. Everyone inside the castle would support the fighting: lads from the kitchens would bring up bundles of new arrows, maid servants would look after the wounded, and monks would apply dressings and medicines made from herbs in the castle gardens.

Women tend the wounded

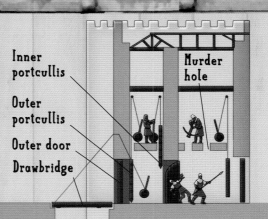

Inner portcullis

Murder hole

Outer portcullis

Outer door

Drawbridge

Gatehouse defences

If an attacker managed to enter the castle gate house, he could be trapped between the inner and the outer portcullis. Defenders could drop hot sand or burning wood on him through the "murder holes".

9

The siege:
Day 23

It's raining rain and raining arrows, too. We're exhausted from digging, chopping down trees and shifting stones. We've filled in parts of the moat. Now we can get close to the castle walls and put up the ladders. At last we can fight the enemy hand to hand!

Batter and bash

Attackers sometimes built a wheeled shelter called a sow. This protected them from arrows as they filled in parts of the moat, and let them move forward to the foot of the castle walls. They raised ladders and climbed up to fight on the battlements; they wheeled up battering rams and tall siege towers.

Mobile towers

The attackers wheeled the belfries up to the walls. They were filled with archers, crossbowmen and assault troops armed with swords or pikes. Thick hide (animal skins) on the sides of the tower protected the soldiers.

Belfry

The attackers built tall scaffolding towers called belfries up to the height of the castle wall, or even a bit higher. The sides were daubed with wet mud, so that they would not catch fire.

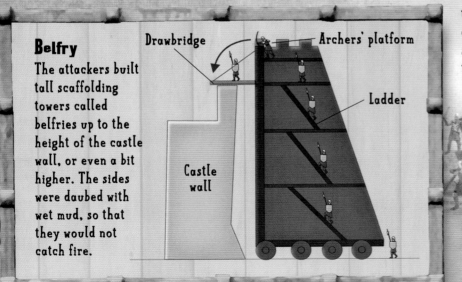

Drawbridge

Archers' platform

Ladder

Castle wall

Belfry

Scaling ladders

Climbing the walls was deadly dangerous. The ladders could be easily tipped over, and defenders could attack the climbers with arrows, stones or boiling water.

Open the gates!

If assault troops got inside the castle, the fighting was fierce. But with luck, a group might reach the gate and open it to their soldiers.

Battering ram

The battering ram was a tree trunk or massive timber, sometimes with an iron tip. It hung from chains or ropes inside the wheeled frame. The ram was swung against a gate or a weak part of the wall, in order to smash a way through.

Scaling ladders

Battering ram

Fling and sling

Weapons engineers built giant catapults before a war or siege began. In England, many were made at the Tower of London. The parts were stored in royal castles or cities around the country. They could then be shipped or hauled to the siege by ox-cart, and assembled on the spot under the instruction of experts.

The siege:
Day 32

We're just about holding off the attackers, but food is running out. Part of the King's army has moved away, but we think they're off to fight a relief force being sent by our allies. Their chief engineer has arrived with new machines of destruction – God help us all!

Sling

Stone ball

Mangonel

Ballista

Ballista

A kind of giant crossbow, the ballista was designed to kill troops rather than smash walls. Its string, made of twisted sinew (animal tendons), was winched back, then released to fire darts. A smaller version, the springald, could be used for fighting inside castles.

Mangonel

A typical mangonel had a single arm attached to a powerful oak beam and frame. It was powered by twisted ropes. The operators winched back the arm and loaded it with a ball of stone. When released, the arm sprang back up against the crossbar, releasing its killer load.

Trebuchet

The trebuchet was the ultimate catapult. It had a long arm with a sling at the end. The first trebuchets used muscle power to haul back the firing arm. From the 1100s, engineers used a heavy counterweight. This made the arm shoot violently forward when it was released, and lob the missile high over the castle walls.

Arm

Supports

Wooden box full of stones to act as counterweight

Carved stone balls

Ammunition

Trebuchets and mangonels could fire stones, boulders, or barrels of burning tar. At the siege of Kafa in 1346, attackers catapulted dead bodies infected by the plague over the walls.

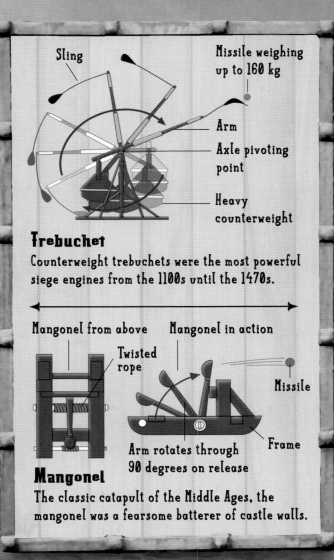

Sling

Missile weighing up to 160 kg

Arm

Axle pivoting point

Heavy counterweight

Trebuchet

Counterweight trebuchets were the most powerful siege engines from the 1100s until the 1470s.

Mangonel from above

Twisted rope

Mangonel in action

Missile

Frame

Arm rotates through 90 degrees on release

Mangonel

The classic catapult of the Middle Ages, the mangonel was a fearsome batterer of castle walls.

We defeated the forces that were marching to relieve the castle, then a lucky shot with a trebuchet brought part of the wall down. Our men-at-arms swarmed through, made it to the gate house and let down the drawbridge – we're in at last! Sir Hugh was led away in chains: victory is ours!

The castle falls

It was often easier to defend a castle than to attack it. Even so, a large army that had money, time, manpower and siege engines could be victorious. By the 1470s warfare was changing: guns could now pound thick walls into rubble. The age of castles was coming to an end.

Storm the breach

At this stage defenders would be hungry and desperate and, when the attackers broke through, they would often be outnumbered. Many would die defending the keep. Flames would bring timbers crashing down – and the siege would be over at last.

Early cannon designs

Cannon were first used in Europe in the early 1300s. At first they were unreliable. They often blew up and killed the gunners instead of the enemy. After the 1450s, the design of cannon improved. Castles were no longer safe.

Bottle cannon 1350

Ottoman cannon 1453

Still standing

Gunpowder helped to bring about the end of castles. So did big social and economic changes. Lords and ladies now preferred to live in fancy palaces than in draughty, smelly castles. The many castles that still stand today remind us of the days of knights, archers, mangonels and trebuchets.

Real sieges of the Middle Ages

Acre •

1189–91 Acre
Location: Modern Akko, Israel
Duration: 683 days
Defending: Ayyubid Muslims
Garrison: 6,000
Relief army: 8,000
Commander: Saladin
Attacking: Christian Crusaders
Numbers: About 25,000
Outcome: Crusader victory

• Kiev

1240 Kiev
Location: Ukraine
Duration: 8 days
Defending: Halych-Volhynia
Commander: Voivode Dmytro
Numbers: About 1,000
Attacking: Large army of Mongols
Commander: Batu Khan
Outcome: Mongol victory

Build your own mangonel

Imagine you are a medieval Master of the Royal Engines. Make this infernal mangonel to confound the foe. Give it a name to strike terror in all who see it in action – the Thunderer, the Mouth of Hell or the Castle Shaker!

All the pieces are numbered. All the tabs, slots and other joining places are marked with letters to help you to match them.

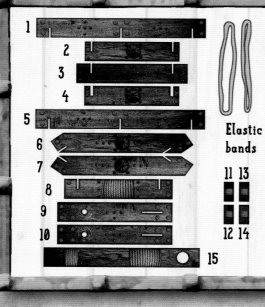

Elastic bands

1

Take piece 1 and slot it into piece 2 at a, into piece 3 at b, and into piece 4 at c.

2

Slot piece 5 into piece 2 at f, into 3 at e, and into 4 at d.

3

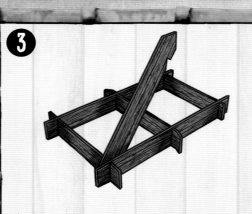

Slot piece 6 into piece 2 at f, making sure piece 6 is on the inside of the frame.

4

Slot piece 7 into piece 2 at a, making sure piece 7 is on the inside of the frame.

5 Slot piece 8 into piece 6 at g, and into piece 7 at h.

6 Attach piece 9 to piece 8 at i, making sure that the numbers are facing inward.

7 Attach piece 10 to piece 8 at j, making sure that the numbers are facing inward.

8 Slot pieces 11 and 12 together at k to form a cross. Do the same with pieces 13 and 14 at l.

9 Push both elastic bands through the hole at m ...

10 ... and out of the hole at n. It's a tight fit, so squeeze the bands together with your fingers to push them through the hole.

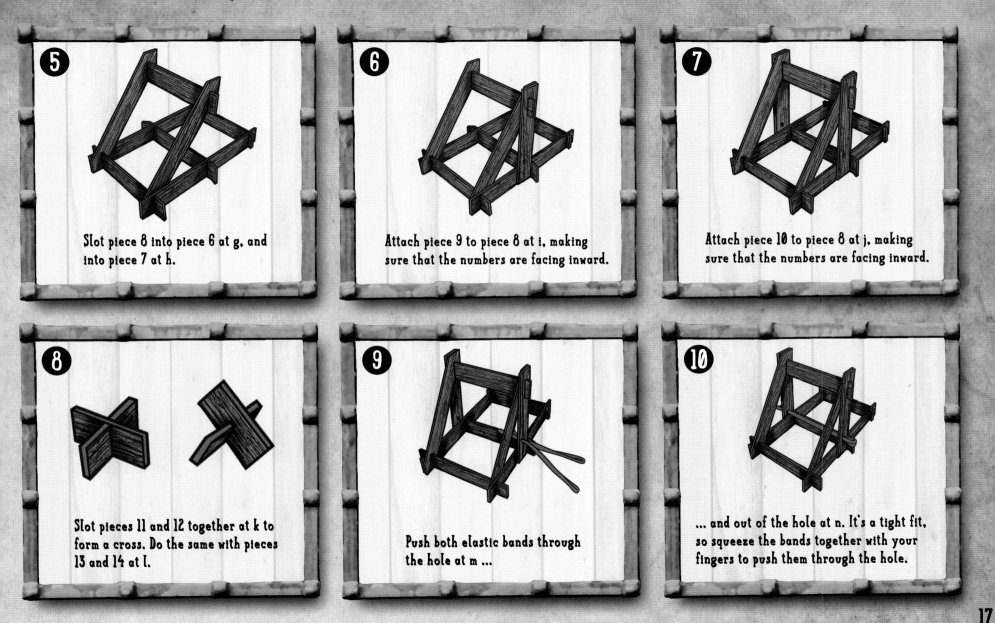

11

Take the end of one elastic band at hole m, and stretch it over the cross made by pieces 11 and 12. Repeat this step on the other side of the model at hole n, using the cross made by pieces 13 and 14.

12

Take the end of the other elastic band at hole m and loop it around the cross in the other direction, so that it crosses over the first loop. Repeat on the other side.

13

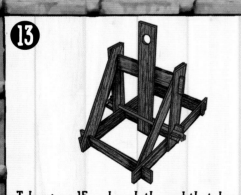

Take piece 15 and push the end that doesn't have a hole between the two elastic bands in the centre.

14

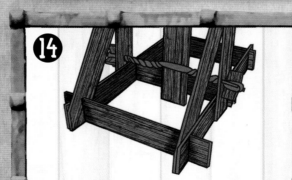

Take hold of both crosses and turn them clockwise at the same time to twist the elastic bands. Keep winding until the elastic bands are twisted as tightly as possible.

Position your targets

Press out the targets and slot the semicircular "feet" on to the bottom of each one. Stand them about a metre away from your mangonel.

Ammunition

Take a square of paper – A5 size or 20 x 15 cm works well. Roll it into a ball big enough to rest in the hole at the end of piece 15. You could pile up a stock of missiles for quick reloading.

Take aim ...

Pull back the mangonel arm and hold it steady while you load your paper missile in the hole.

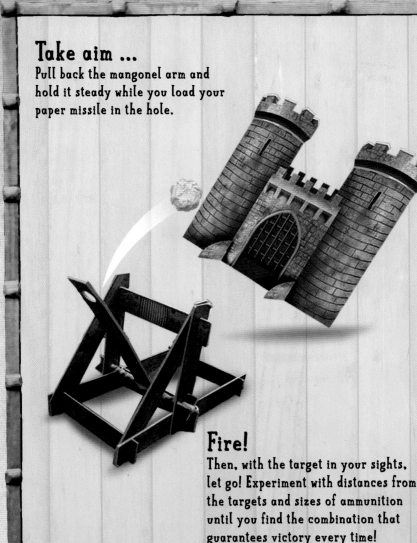

Fire!

Then, with the target in your sights, let go! Experiment with distances from the targets and sizes of ammunition until you find the combination that guarantees victory every time!

Mangonel repair

Specialist engineers called ingeniators built and repaired siege engines. The word ingeniator means someone who is ingenious or clever.

If a siege engine broke down on the battlefield, how long it took to fix depended on the nature of the fault, the number of carpenters that were on hand, and whether the right spare parts had been brought along. A complicated break could take months to repair, but a lash-up with a spare bit of timber might take just a couple of hours.

The most likely battle repair you (or your ingeniator) will have to deal with is a broken band. If a band breaks, you'll need to find a replacement of a similar strength and length, then follow the steps opposite from number 11.

May your siege end in victory!

Glossary

arbalest A crossbow, especially a larger, more powerful version with a steel bow.

bailey The fortified outer court of a castle.

ballista A large engine of war based on the crossbow principle. Originally used in ancient Greece and Rome, it was still in use in the Middle Ages.

battering ram A heavy log or beam used to weaken and break down castle gates or walls. It could be carried on, and swung from, chains.

belfry Literally a bell tower, but the word also describes the siege tower, a high wooden scaffolding protected by animal hides (skins). It was wheeled up to the castle walls for an assault.

cavalry Mounted troops.

counterweight A weight used to balance another one. Its equal and opposing force could be used to propel the arm of a trebuchet.

drawbridge A bridge that can be raised to prevent access or lowered to let people in or out.

glaive Any pole weapon with a head shaped like a knife or sword. At times also used to describe lances, swords and large daggers.

halberd A two-handed pole weapon mounted with an axe blade and a spike.

heraldry The system of emblems, colours and patterns originally used to identify knights, nobles or royalty. These would appear on shields and surcoats, becoming known as coats-of-arms.

hide Tough animal skin, leather.

hoarding A wooden gallery fixed to castle walls during a siege. This gave the defenders better lines of fire and allowed them to attack people directly underneath.

keep A tower or stronghold within a castle's defensive walls.

kettle helmet A steel helmet in the shape of a hat with a brim, worn by infantry.

longbow A tall bow, drawn by hand and used to fire arrows.

mail A fabric made from closely interlocking rings of iron or steel, used as armour.

mantlet A portable structure used to protect archers from hostile fire. A large shield was called a pavise.

moat A deep and wide defensive ditch, surrounding a castle. It was often filled with water.

motte A defensive mound, topped by a defensive structure such as a tower.

ox cart A wagon pulled by an ox (a cow or bull), or by oxen (more than one ox).

palisade A defensive wooden fence.

parley To negotiate, or hold a conference. Also the conference itself.

pole axe A long pole fitted with an axe blade.

portcullis A strong metal or timber grille that could be lowered to seal off a castle under attack.

quilted armour Armour made of padded cloth rather than of leather or metal.

siege engine Any large machine, such as a catapult, used during a siege.

sortie An attack made by troops coming out from a defensive position; a counterattack launched from a castle.

span The distance between two tips.

springald A type of small ballista, with arms that swing inwards.

stirrup A metal or rope foothold, suspended from the saddle of a horse. It gives the rider stability and leverage.

tiller The shaft or stock of a crossbow.

ward An inner or outer walled area of a castle.